HISTORY DETECTIVES

ANCIENT GREECE

HISTORY DETECTIVES

ANCIENT GREECE

WRITTEN BY PHILIP ARDAGH
ILLUSTRATED BY COLIN KING

PETER BEDRICK BOOKS
NTC/Contemporary Publishing Group
NEW YORK

First published in the United States of America in 2000
by Peter Bedrick Books
a division of NTC/Contemporary Publishing Group
4255 West Touhy Avenue
Lincolnwood (Chicago), Illinois, 60712-1975, USA

ISBN 0-87226-630-3

Text copyright © Macmillan Children's Books 2000
Illustrations copyright © Colin King 2000
Border artwork by Sally Taylor

Philip Ardagh and Colin King have asserted their right to be
identified as the Author and Illustrator of this Work in accordance
with the Copyright, Designs and Patents Act of the United Kingdom 1988.

1 3 5 7 9 8 6 4 2

Printed in Singapore

The publishers would like to thank the following for their permission to use the photographic material reproduced in this book.

a = above, b = below, c = centre, l = left, r = right

Opening page:British Museum, London/Michael Holford; Title page: British Museum, London, British Museum, London/Michael Holford,
Ancient Art & Architecture Collection, British Museum, London; 10a: British Museum, London/Michael Holford; 10b: Ancient Art & Architecture
Collection; 11a Capitoline Museum, Rome/E.T Archive; 11b: National Archaeological Museum, Naples/ E.T Archive; 13a: Dr. S. Coyne/Ancient Art
& Architecture Collection; 13b: Roy Rainford/Robert Harding Picture Library; 15: Louvre, Paris/ Erich Lessing/AKG, London; 17: British Museum/Michael
Holford; 19a & b: Ancient Art & Architecture Collection; 21a & b: Ancient Art & Architecture Collection; 23a: British Museum, London; 23b: Ancient Art &
Architecture Collection; 25a & B: Ancient Art & Architecture Collection; 27a: Michael Holford; 27b: Ancient Art & Architecture Collection; 29a & b:
Michael Holford; 31a: Robert Harding Picture Library; 31b: Ancient Art & Architecture Collection; 33a: Ancient Art & Architecture Collection; 33b: Scala;
35a: Hirmer Archiv; 35b: Ancient Art & Architecture Collection; 37a & b: British Museum, London; 38a & b: AKG, London; 39a & b: AKG, London;
40a & b: Ancient Art & Architecture Collection; 41a: Ancient art & Architecture Collection; 41b: Michael Holford; 42: Roy Rainford/Robert Harding
Picture Library; Ancient Art & Architecture Collection; 43: Ancient Art & Architecture Collection, Michael Holford.

CONTENTS

ANCIENT GREECE

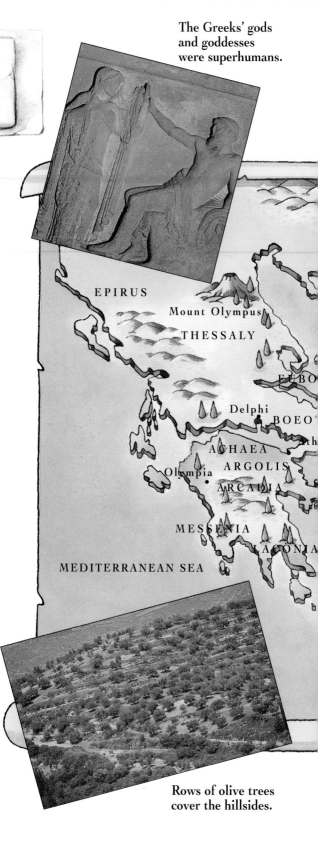

The Greeks' gods and goddesses were superhumans.

Ancient Greece wasn't a single country but included many different islands and part of the mainland. There was no single ruler or government and each Greek state had different laws. Occasionally they united against common enemies but, more often, fought amongst themselves.

THE FIRST GREEKS

The first Greeks lived about 40,000 years ago, but farming and building didn't begin until about 8,000 years ago. The first major Greek society was on the island of Crete. The Minoans flourished there between 2200BC and 1450BC until their towns were destroyed by fire. On the mainland, people called the Mycenaeans prospered from about 1600BC to 1100BC.

THE DARK AGES

Next came the Dark Ages from c.1100BC to 800BC, a time when many of the skills of the past were lost, including the art of writing — so no written records exist to tell us what happened. The Mycenaeans were overrun, but we don't know who by!

Rows of olive trees cover the hillsides.

8

Vases show scenes from Greek life.

THE ARCHAIC PERIOD

Historians call the next period in Ancient Greek history the Archaic Period, a time of prosperity and the rebirth of civilization. It was during these 300 years (c.800BC to 500BC) that Greece became a collection of city states, called *poleis*. These included Athens, Sparta, Thebes, Corinth and Argos. It was also during this period that hundreds of Greek colonies were set up, along with trading posts, in places such as Egypt, Spain, Syria and Turkey. There were so many colonies in what we now call Italy and Sicily that the area once had the nickname "Greater Greece"!

THE CLASSICAL PERIOD AND THE HELLENISTIC AGE

The Classical Period (480BC to 336BC) is what many people think of as the "golden age" of Ancient Greece. Magnificent cities and temples were built, and much of what we think of as being typically Ancient Greek comes from this period. Greece grew rich and the arts and sciences blossomed, despite a 27-year war between Athens and Sparta. Later, Alexander the Great of Macedonia created a huge empire, which included Greece and its territories. Finally came the Hellenistic Age from 336BC to 30BC. After 146BC, Ancient Greece gradually found itself under the control of the Romans, as part of the growing Roman Empire.

DISCOVERY

This bust of Homer is simply the sculptor's idea of what the poet might have looked like. It was made long after Homer's time. In the same way, Homer wrote about the Trojan Wars at least 400 years after they were supposed to have happened.

This Roman mosaic shows a Roman soldier about to murder Archimedes who, as an inhabitant of the city of Syracuse, was officially an enemy of Rome. The killing was against the wishes of Marcellus, the Roman general in charge.

FAMOUS NAMES

Much of what we know about the very early so-called history of Ancient Greece comes from the poet Homer. He wrote about events in the Trojan War (see pages 38 & 39) in two epic poems called *The Iliad* and *The Odyssey*, but it's hard to tell if these are fact or fiction, or even a blend of the two. In the same way, little is known about Homer himself. He is thought to have lived in the 9th century BC and may have been blind. His stories were passed on by word of mouth, and weren't written down until centuries later.

INVENTIONS

Much more is known about the inventor, mathematician and astronomer Archimedes (c.287BC-212BC) but, again, legend has grown up around him. He is said to have built giant mirrors that could deflect the sun's rays onto enemy ships and burn them. He is also supposed to have constructed giant claw-like cranes that could lift invading ships right out of the water. He is probably most famous for jumping out of a bath of water with the cry "Eureka!", which means "I've found it!" He had just worked out an important law of physics.

THE IDEAS MEN

Ancient Greece produced a great many thinkers, including Socrates and Plato. Socrates (c.469BC-399BC) came from Athens. At a time when most scholars were writing down their ideas, Socrates preferred to talk about his, and teach them in person. His ideas soon got him into trouble with the government of Athens. He was sentenced to death by drinking the poison hemlock. The "wrong" sort of ideas were seen as a dangerous weapon.

Plato (c. 429BC-347BC) had been one of Socrates's pupils and fled Athens after his teacher's death. He later returned and wrote *The Apology*, to try to answer the people who criticized Socrates's ideas. Plato set up a world-famous school called the Academy, which carried on teaching his ideas long after his death.

HISTORIES

Thucydides (c.460BC-369BC) is famous as the first true historian. His account of the 27-year war between Athens and Sparta, called the Peloponnesian War, is considered to be the first real history book.

ALEXANDER THE GREAT

Alexander the Great (356BC-323BC) didn't write about battles. He fought them. When his father, King Philip of Macedonia — who had already conquered Ancient Greece and its colonies — was murdered, many thought that Alexander, only 20 years old, was too young to take the throne. He proved them wrong. He was a brilliant general and a brave fighter. He invaded the empire of the Persian king, Darius III, and created the biggest empire the world had ever known. When Alexander died at 33, he had been ruler of almost the entire world known to the Ancient Greeks.

DISCOVERY

This carving is of Plato. Plato's school was closed by the Roman emperor Justinian in AD529. When Greece became part of the Roman Empire, the Romans copied or used many Greek ideas, from art and architecture to technology and sciences. Justinian was a Christian, however, and Plato's teachings were seen to be against Christian beliefs.

The city of Alexandria in Egypt was founded and named after Alexander the Great, who is shown here in the heat of battle, on this Roman mosaic.

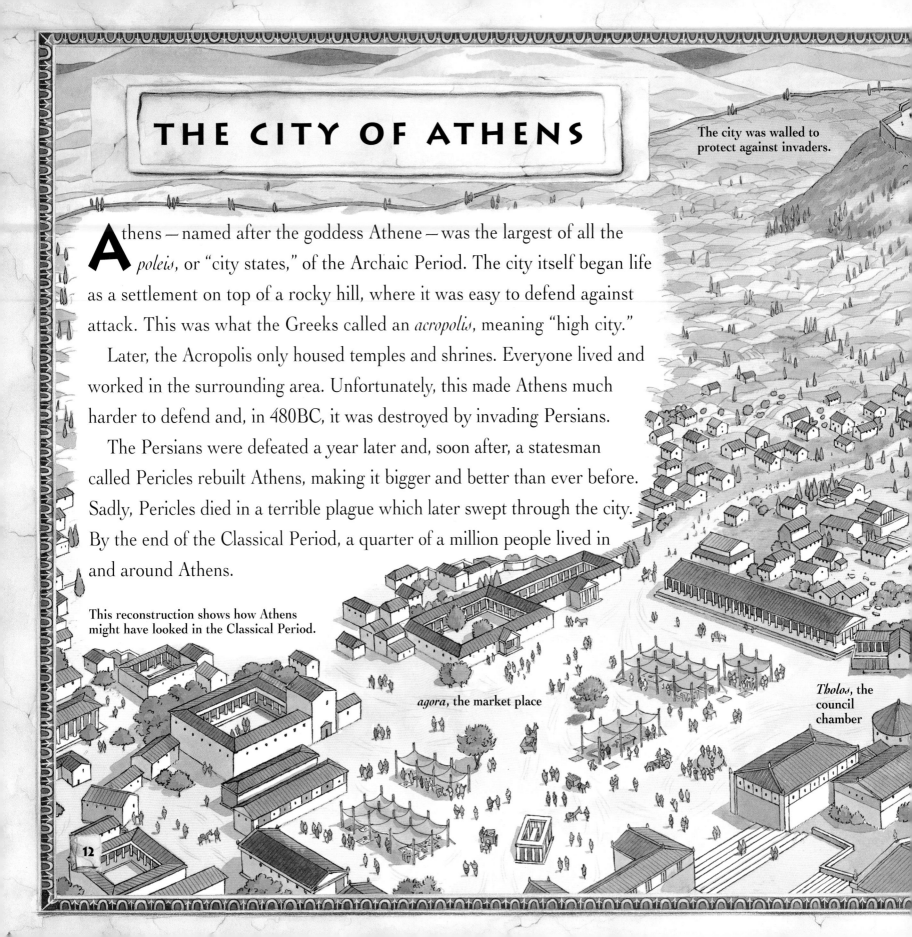

THE CITY OF ATHENS

The city was walled to protect against invaders.

Athens — named after the goddess Athene — was the largest of all the *poleis*, or "city states," of the Archaic Period. The city itself began life as a settlement on top of a rocky hill, where it was easy to defend against attack. This was what the Greeks called an *acropolis*, meaning "high city."

Later, the Acropolis only housed temples and shrines. Everyone lived and worked in the surrounding area. Unfortunately, this made Athens much harder to defend and, in 480BC, it was destroyed by invading Persians.

The Persians were defeated a year later and, soon after, a statesman called Pericles rebuilt Athens, making it bigger and better than ever before. Sadly, Pericles died in a terrible plague which later swept through the city. By the end of the Classical Period, a quarter of a million people lived in and around Athens.

This reconstruction shows how Athens might have looked in the Classical Period.

agora, the market place

Tholos, the council chamber

12

The Parthenon was built by Ictinus between 447BC and 438BC.

the Propylaea — gateway to the "sacred enclosure"

Acropolis

Panathenaic Way — the road to the Acropolis

Houses were plain with pottery roof tiles and bare white walls.

wall hangings added color

mosaic pebble floor

DISCOVERY

According to myth, Athene and the sea god Poseidon argued over the naming of the city. They decided to let the people choose. Poseidon offered them riches with trade across the seas. Athene offered an olive tree. The people chose her gift, because olive oil has so many uses. They named the city "Athens" after her. This statue of Poseidon is missing his trident, a three-pronged spear.

One of the most famous sights in Athens today is this, the ruins of the Parthenon. It was a temple built to the glory of the goddess Athene and is seen here from the west.

GODS AND GODDESSES

Some of the most important Greek gods and goddesses are shown here.

Worshipping gods and goddesses was an important part of daily life in Ancient Greece. They were said to look and behave like "superhumans," though some were thought to be able to change shape. Myths and legends about Ancient Greek gods and goddesses are still famous all over the world.

Despite this, some of their names seem unfamiliar. That's because the Romans later "stole" the Greek gods and gave them their own names! For example, the Greek mythical hero Heracles—who earned the right to be a god—is better known by the Roman name, Hercules.

Hermes, Messenger to the Gods

Ares, God of War

Athene, Goddess of Wisdom and War

Poseidon, God of the Seas

Pluto, King of the Underworld

Hestia, Goddess of the Hearth

14

Artemis, Goddess
of the Moon

Zeus, King of the Gods

Hera, Queen
of Gods,
sister and
wife of Zeus

Aphrodite,
Goddess of Love
and Beauty

Demeter,
Goddess of
Plants and
Agriculture

Apollo, God
of Light and
Truth (plus
poetry and
music)

Dionysus, God
of Wine and
Fertility

DISCOVERY

The Greeks believed in life after death. According to these beliefs, a dead person's soul was guided to the underworld by Hermes. It then had to be rowed across the River Styx by Charon, the ferryman. On the other bank, the soul was greeted by Cerberus, Pluto's three-headed guard dog.

Next, the soul was judged. Souls of cruel people were sent to Tartarus, for never-ending punishment. Most people went to the Asphodel Fields. The souls of people who had been good in life, or were members of mystery cults (see page 16) were sent to the Elysian Fields — a place of sunshine and laughter.

Souls of mystery cult members could ask to be born again. If they led three good lives, and were sent to the Elysian fields three times, they could then go to the Isles of the Blessed, a paradise.

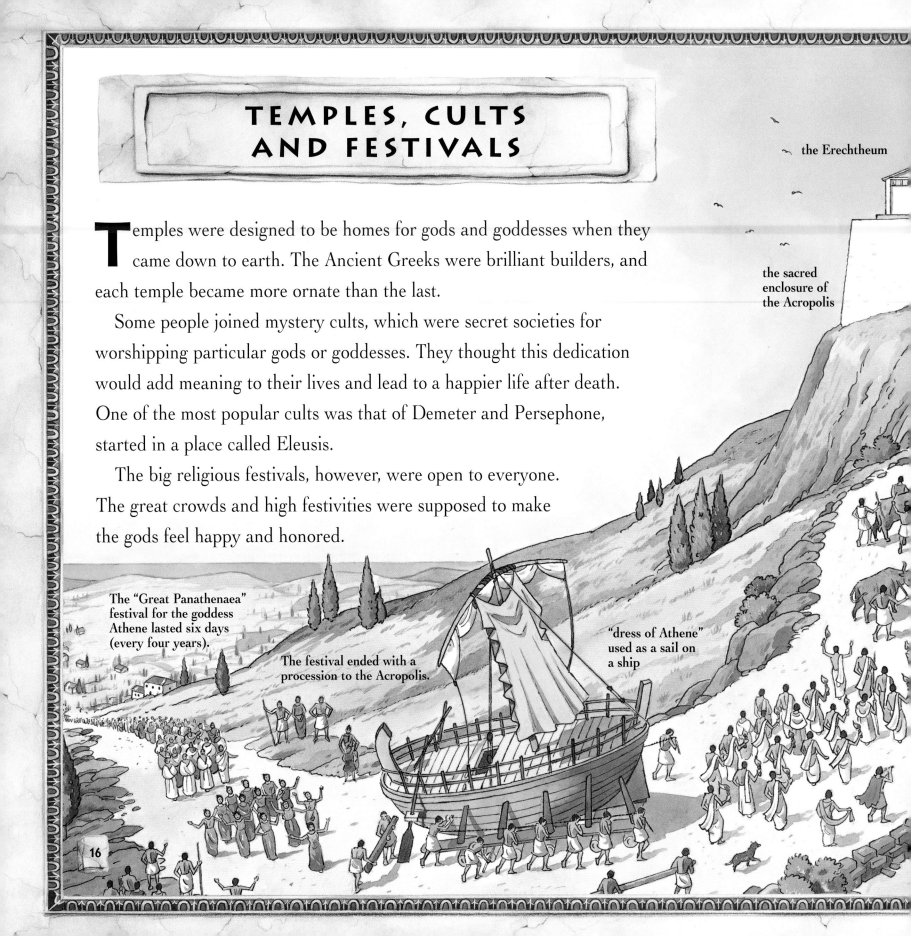

TEMPLES, CULTS AND FESTIVALS

~ the Erechtheum

Temples were designed to be homes for gods and goddesses when they came down to earth. The Ancient Greeks were brilliant builders, and each temple became more ornate than the last.

Some people joined mystery cults, which were secret societies for worshipping particular gods or goddesses. They thought this dedication would add meaning to their lives and lead to a happier life after death. One of the most popular cults was that of Demeter and Persephone, started in a place called Eleusis.

The big religious festivals, however, were open to everyone. The great crowds and high festivities were supposed to make the gods feel happy and honored.

the sacred enclosure of the Acropolis

The "Great Panathenaea" festival for the goddess Athene lasted six days (every four years).

The festival ended with a procession to the Acropolis.

"dress of Athene" used as a sail on a ship

16

the Propylaea gateway

the Parthenon — the most famous of Greek temples

Nike, Goddess of Victory

a 40-foot high statue of Athene, made from gold and ivory

animals for sacrifice

Myth has it that the goddess Demeter had a daughter called Persephone. Pluto fell in love with her, seized her and took her down to his kingdom of the dead.

While Demeter, Goddess of Plants and Agriculture, hunted for Persephone, she allowed the crops to die.

When Demeter found out where Persephone was, Zeus agreed to free her providing Persephone hadn't eaten anything in the Underworld.

As a result, Pluto then tricked her into eating six pomegranate seeds. Despite this, Zeus let Persephone return to her mother, but made certain conditions. Each year, Persephone must spend a month with Pluto for every seed she had eaten.

So for six months, Persephone was with Demeter, bringing her happiness and letting the crops grow. For six months she was with Pluto, and Demeter was sad. Plants and crops died. That, says the story, is how we come to have summer and winter.

17

DOCTORS AND MEDICINE

According to myth, Asclepius was the son of the god Apollo, but was brought up by a centaur (half man/half horse). The centaur taught Asclepius the secrets of medicine and he became the God of Healing. The first Greek "doctors" were actually priests of Asclepius.

Often ill people slept inside the temples, hoping to be cured or to have dreams of how to be cured.

Some doctors didn't believe in the religious explanations for illness. They looked for other causes of disease. A new movement was founded by a man called Hippocrates. His doctors not only provided medicine, but were also aware of the importance of diet, rest and exercise.

They even carried out operations but without anesthetics or antiseptics. These were very painful and dangerous and most patients died.

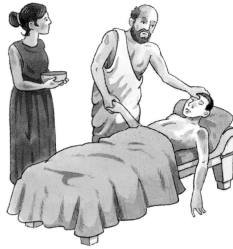

Later, doctors following Hippocrates examined patients for clues to their illnesses.

People thought illness was a punishment from the gods, and the priests tried to help them.

Sick people then had to perform ceremonies, but some were also offered medicines.

Those cured gave thanks and offerings.

Medicines were made from herbs.

surgical instruments

Asclepius's staff was always shown with a snake, or snakes, entwined around it, as it is here. The staff is now used as a symbol by many medical organizations throughout the world. "The Hippocratic Oath," sworn by doctors to care for their patients, is named after Hippocrates.

This strange relief carving was given as an offering of thanks to Asclepius, by someone who believed that their leg had been cured by the god.

19

THE RULE OF THE PEOPLE

The Council met in the *Tholos*. There were 500 councillors altogether.

At the end of the Archaic Period, some city states overthrew their absolute rulers, the *tyrants*. Instead, they set up governments by the people for the people. This type of rule was called democracy, from the Greek words *demos* meaning "people" and *kratos* meaning "rule." All citizens now had a say. Ancient Greek society was divided into two main groups: free people, and slaves (who were usually foreign). In Athens, free men were divided into two further groups: citizens and *metics*. Citizens had full rights and full responsibilities. *Metics* were citizens from other states. A woman simply took on the social status of her husband or father.

At the start of the Archaic Period, the rich land-owning aristocrats ruled most states (*aristoi* means "best people"). Then came the *tyrants* in about 650BC. Democracy finally reached Athens in 508BC.

The Assembly met every ten days.

When democracy first came to Athens, citizens were divided into small communities, called *demes*.

Demes were then grouped together into larger units called *trittyes*:

10 city *trittyes*	10 country *trittyes*	10 coastal *trittyes*

a phyle

1 city *trittyes*, 1 country *trittyes* and 1 coastal *trittyes* made up a phyle. There were 10 *phylai* or "tribes" in all.

In a trial in Athens there were no judges or lawyers.

They processed laws to put before the Assembly.

These laws were suggested by citizens.

The Assembly met on a hill called the Pnyx.

Citizens voted for or against suggestions passed through the Council.

The jurors themselves — 200 or more — made the decisions.

DISCOVERY

Unpopular politicians could be removed by vote. The unpopular man's name was scratched onto a piece of broken pottery, such as this, called an *ostrakon*. If a man's name appeared often enough he could be banished. This is where the word "ostracize" comes from, meaning "to exclude" or "banish."

These are ballot discs, used by jurors to record their verdicts. If a juror felt the accused was innocent, he handed in a disc with a stalk. If he thought the person guilty, he turned in one with a hole in the middle.

21

THE ARMY AND NAVY

A typical trireme was about 40 meters (135ft) long.

At the start of the Archaic Period, every soldier had to pay for his own armor and weapons, however poor he was. This meant that ordinary foot soldiers were badly equipped. What little strength the army had came from the aristocrats, who made up the cavalry. They were the only people who could afford horses and proper armor!

Trade changed this. As Ancient Greece grew richer from trading with other countries, the middle classes could afford good quality armor and weaponry. These new, better-equipped soldiers were called *hoplites*.

In the navy, warships relied on manpower as well as windpower — with oars as well as sails — so many poorer free men could serve as oarsmen. They didn't have to buy expensive armor. The most effective type of war-ship was a trireme with oarsmen at three different levels on both sides. It was very big and very fast.

The front of a trireme was rammed into enemy warships.

The armies of Athens were led by commanders called *strategoi*.

In Athens, all men did two years' military training.

22

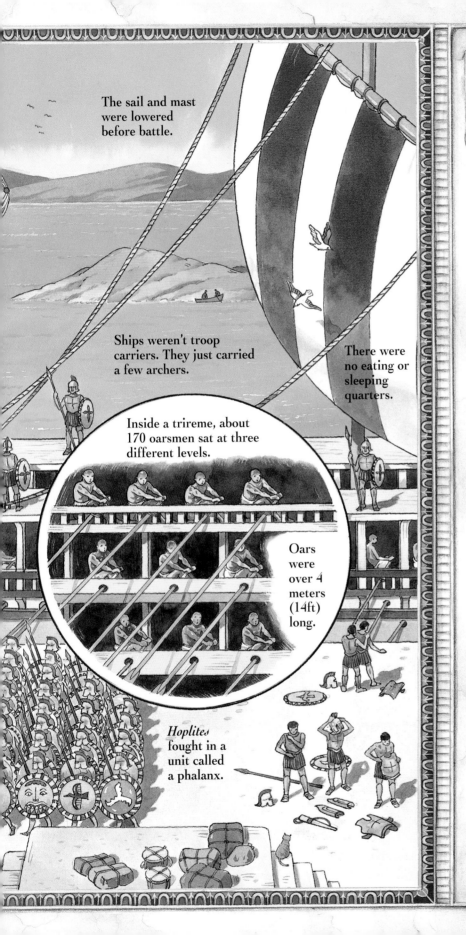

The sail and mast were lowered before battle.

Ships weren't troop carriers. They just carried a few archers.

There were no eating or sleeping quarters.

Inside a trireme, about 170 oarsmen sat at three different levels.

Oars were over 4 meters (14ft) long.

Hoplites fought in a unit called a phalanx.

DISCOVERY

Archaeologists have to be careful when studying ancient pictures for clues. This painting, on a vase, appears to show a ship with oarsmen on two levels. In fact, the men on the "upper" level are really the oarsmen on the far side, sitting *next* to those at the "bottom" front.

This relief carving shows a group of typical *hoplites*, or Greek foot soldiers, with their distinctive high-plumed helmets and big round shields.

23

SPORTS AND GAMES

At Olympia, up to 4000 spectators could watch a race.

The Greeks took their sport very seriously, especially athletics. Even when the city states were at war with each other, they would have a truce during their official competitions, called games. Different games were held in honor of different gods. For example, the Isthmian Games were held in Corinth in honor of Poseidon, while the Pythian Games at Delphi were held in honor of Apollo.

wrestling

The most famous of these was the Olympic Games, first held at Olympia, in honor of Zeus, in 776BC. This was a place in southern Greece, and not Mount Olympus where the gods and goddesses were thought to live. The Olympic Games, which were held every four years, were finally banned by the Roman emperor Theodosius in AD394. He was a Christian and didn't like the idea of the competition honoring the king of the Greek gods.

The most popular Olympic event was chariot racing.

Chariots were pulled by two or four horses.

Chariot racing was a very dangerous sport and many drivers often died in high speed crashes.

Athletes ran with their heavy helmets and heavy shields.

In the long jump competition, jumpers swung weights to carry them further.

Winners were given "crowns" of olive leaves, leather or even gold.

DISCOVERY

There was a public holiday while the Olympic Games were held. This meant thousands of people could go and watch. This marble statue shows a competitor about to throw a discus. Winning competitions was an honor for the winners' cities as well as for themselves. There were no real prizes, just the glory of victory.

Women weren't allowed to take part in any games except for the Heraia. These were held in honor of the goddess Hera, shown here with her husband Zeus. There were only three women's events, all running races.

THE THEATER

The idea for what we know now as "theater" came from Ancient Greece. The first theatrical events were part of a religious festival honoring the god Dionysus, which was celebrated throughout the countryside. This then became the City Dionysia festival, held in Athens. It included many songs, dances and competitions.

Originally these were performed in the *agora* or market place. Later an open-air theater was built on the slopes of the Acropolis. This was the first building especially built for the unique purpose of performance. Soon theaters spread across the whole Greek world.

The very first plays were about gods and were performed by a singing and dancing chorus. Later, one or two actors took part. Finally, a playwright called Sophocles wrote plays involving many actors, like we have today.

Theaters could seat up to 20,000 people.

A flying rig (a wooden crane) was used to make actors "fly."

The chorus entered through the *parodos*.

Actors wore masks.

The audience sat on stone seats.

altar to Dionysus

All singing and dancing took place here, in the area known as the *orchestra*.

26

Characters "killed" off-stage could be rolled out of the *skene* and shown on a kind of bed called an *ekkyklema*.

At the back of the stage was a building called the *skene*.

Scenery was painted on the front.

Actors stood on the proscenium.

chorus

Masks made it easy to tell characters apart, even from the back of the audience.

DISCOVERY

Some Ancient Greek theaters are still used to stage special performances today, including this fine example in Epidauros.

This statue shows a Greek comic actor wearing a smiling mask. Greek theaters were huge, so masks helped characters to be recognized more easily from a distance.

SCULPTURE, MUSIC AND POETRY

This is a reconstruction of a dinner party inside an *andron* (dining room).

Classical Period statues

The Ancient Greeks loved statues and put them in temples, homes and public places. Music was everywhere too, not only at festivals and celebrations, but as a part of training for soldiers and sailors. There were even drinking songs! Poetry was equally popular. It was said to be the gift of the god Apollo, and was usually read aloud by *rhapsodes*.

Early in the Archaic Period, statues looked stiff and formal and were based on Egyptian styles. Over time, they became far more realistic. By the Classical Period, the trend was for statues of mighty gods and goddesses. In the Hellenistic Age, there was more variety and realism.

As well as marble, the Greeks used bronze to make statues — using molds. Though few Ancient Greek statues survive, the Romans copied them and some are exact replicas of Greek works. Few musical instruments survive either, as many were made of wood and would have rotted.

auloi

syrinx

harp

timpanon

Boys and girls learned music. Many professional musicians were women.

lyre

cymbals

jugglers and acrobats

28

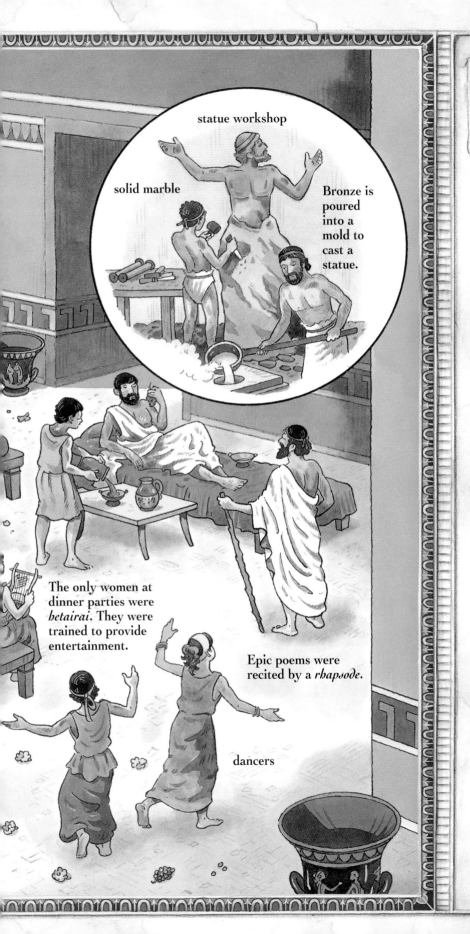

statue workshop

solid marble

Bronze is poured into a mold to cast a statue.

The only women at dinner parties were *hetairai*. They were trained to provide entertainment.

Epic poems were recited by a *rhapsode*.

dancers

DISCOVERY

This part of a bronze statue of Aphrodite, the goddess of love and beauty, was made during the Hellenistic Period. The goddess's hair is shown in what would have been the most fashionable style at the time. Ancient Greek statues were at their most life-like during this period.

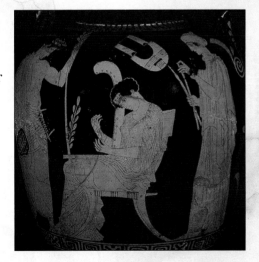

This painting of a group of musicians is from a wine jar dating back to about 440BC. The man is holding a lyre, the seated woman a harp (with her cithara above her), and the woman standing to the left is preparing to play her *auloi* — a pair of pipes.

29

FARMING AND FOOD

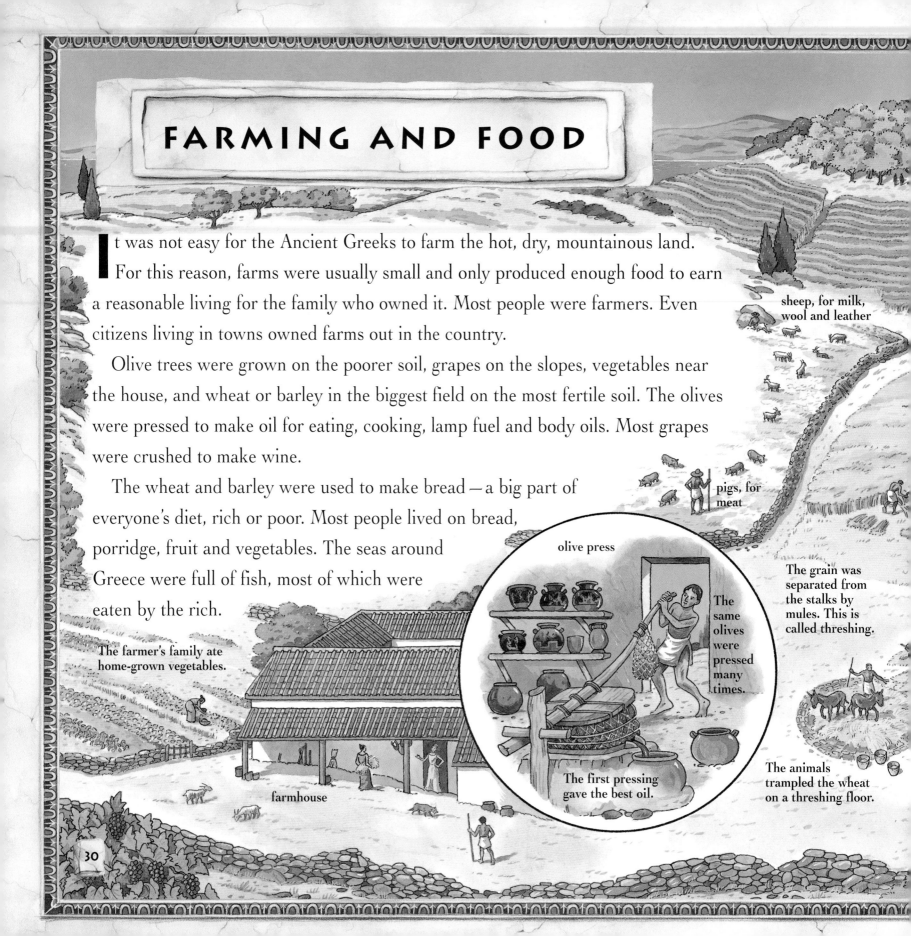

It was not easy for the Ancient Greeks to farm the hot, dry, mountainous land. For this reason, farms were usually small and only produced enough food to earn a reasonable living for the family who owned it. Most people were farmers. Even citizens living in towns owned farms out in the country.

Olive trees were grown on the poorer soil, grapes on the slopes, vegetables near the house, and wheat or barley in the biggest field on the most fertile soil. The olives were pressed to make oil for eating, cooking, lamp fuel and body oils. Most grapes were crushed to make wine.

The wheat and barley were used to make bread — a big part of everyone's diet, rich or poor. Most people lived on bread, porridge, fruit and vegetables. The seas around Greece were full of fish, most of which were eaten by the rich.

sheep, for milk, wool and leather

pigs, for meat

olive press

The same olives were pressed many times.

The grain was separated from the stalks by mules. This is called threshing.

The farmer's family ate home-grown vegetables.

farmhouse

The first pressing gave the best oil.

The animals trampled the wheat on a threshing floor.

olive groves

vineyard

Wheat was harvested by men with sickles, in April or May.

Oxen carried cut grain to the threshing floor.

winnowing

The grain fell to the ground. The rest of the crop was blown away.

The grain was then milled to make flour.

wine vats, used to crush grapes in September

DISCOVERY

Many ancient farming methods are still used in modern day Greece. The "terraced" olive groves of Lesbos, shown here, make the most of every inch of land, however steep.

This scene on the side of this storage jar, made in about 520BC, shows the olive harvest underway. The olives are knocked from the trees with sticks — a process still used today.

SHOPPING AND TRADE

First and foremost, the independent city states traded between each other. They also traded with Greek colonies, which they later used as springboards for trading further afield. Although trading was carried out by private merchants, they still had to pay the state customs duties (taxes).

Greece's main exports were olive oil, wine, statues, metalwork and cloth. Main imports included everything from silks to ivory.

In the heart of every Greek town was the market place, or *agora*. It was made up of "permanent shops" around the edges, in colonnades, and market stalls (and sometimes a slave market) in the center.

Ancient Greeks paid for the goods with coins. Each state had its own currency.

shops

altar

market stalls

slave market on platform (*kyklos*)

This is what an *agora* in a large town or city might have looked like.

colonnades

statues

hot drink stall

Money changers, or *trapezitai*, changed money for a fee.

They became money lenders and bankers.

The idea for coins came from a place called Lydia (in what is now Turkey). They were introduced into Ancient Greece in about 650BC. Each major Greek city issued its own coins. This coin from the 4th century BC shows the head of Athene, goddess of the city of Athens.

Without fridges and freezers at home, Ancient Greek shoppers had to buy their fresh food everyday. This vase shows a scene of a fishmonger with a huge knife, cutting up fish for a customer.

FASHION, CLOTHES AND JEWELS

Greece was, and still is, a very hot country. Most people wore simple clothes such as cloaks or tunics. Originally, these were made from wool, but better trade meant that cooler cotton and silks became available. Not everyone wore shoes, but hats were a must.

Poor men and slaves often just wore loincloths while rich men wore colorful full-length tunics. A woman would wear a basic dress called a *chiton* over which a *himation* could be worn as a shawl or a cloak. Clothing became more figure-hugging as time went on.

Hairstyles changed a great deal too. Men's beards were big and bushy in the Archaic Period, neatly trimmed in the Classical Period, and a very rare sight indeed in the Hellenistic Age. At the same time, women's hair went from being worn loose and straight to up and curled.

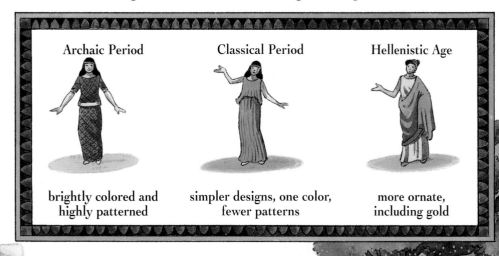

Archaic Period	Classical Period	Hellenistic Age
brightly colored and highly patterned	simpler designs, one color, fewer patterns	more ornate, including gold

a *chlamys*, or short cloak

Classical Period beards were neatly trimmed.

boots

a basic dress, or *chiton*

a *himation* worn here as a shawl

The people in this scene are wearing clothes from the Classical Period.

Slaves wore loincloths.

potter's workshop

Pots for holding scented oils and perfumes were popular with the rich.

a *himation* worn as a traveling cloak

shoes

Only the rich had jewelry made from gold.

Men and women wore hats.

sandals

DISCOVERY

This relief carving shows a Greek woman putting folded clothes into a storage chest. Among the other household items is a bronze mirror, a less ornate version of the type shown below.

This mirror is not made of glass. The Ancient Greek woman who used it would have seen her reflection in the highly polished bronze. Now over 2,000 years old, it has tarnished with time.

35

LIFE AS A CHILD

Most parents in Ancient Greece wanted sons. Some baby girls were actually abandoned by their families, though others were loved and cared for. Ten days after birth, the baby was named during a ceremony called the *amphidromia* in front of the hearth.

Rich families had slaves to act as nannies, bringing up their babies. When they were three, children attended the annual Anthesteria festival of Dionysus and were given special presents.

Only rich families could afford to send their sons to school. Girls, rich or poor, stayed at home. A special slave, called a *paidagogos*, often went with a boy to school to make sure he worked hard.

Schools in Sparta were by far the toughest. The pupils were encouraged to steal food from local farmers to avoid going hungry! This was school policy! It helped to turn out tough soldiers.

The *grammatistes* taught reading, writing and math.

the Ancient Greek alphabet

A B Γ Δ E Z
H Θ I K Λ M
N Ξ O Π P Σ
T Y Φ X Ψ Ω

A birth was announced with a garland on the door of the house — an olive leaf garland for a baby boy, or a woollen garland for a baby girl.

Boys started going to three different schools when they were seven-year-olds, taught by the *grammatistes*, the *kitharistes* and the *paidotribes*.

The *paidotribes* taught physical education — dancing and athletics.

slave nanny

paidagogos

36

Gymnasia soon became more than training grounds and contained libraries and lecture rooms. By the Hellenistic Period, philosophers (thinkers) taught from the *gymnasia* full-time.

The *Paidotribes* often took boys to the gymnasium.

The *kitharistes* taught music and poetry.

DISCOVERY

This pottery pig is a toy rattle. Basic pottery was quite cheap. Even lower-paid parents could afford such toys.

This is a *chous*, a drinking pot which was filled with watered-down wine and given to a three- or four-year-old boy to drink from at the festival of Dionysus. The picture here shows two children playing.

THE SEARCH FOR TROY

The earliest-known picture of the Trojan horse, from a vase dated c. 670BC. If the wooden horse really did exist, it wouldn't have had windows!

Heinrich Schliemann, one of the most famous archeologists of all time.

A legend is a well-known story, based on real people, events or places from the past, which has changed over time. The legend of Troy tells how a man named Paris seized the beautiful Helen of Greece and took her back to the walled city of Troy, which was then besieged by an army of outraged Greek heroes. One day, the people of Troy woke to find the enemy army gone and a huge wooden horse outside the gates. They wheeled the horse into the city and, that night, a group of Greek soldiers who had been hiding inside its belly climbed out and opened the city gates. The Greek army, which had sneaked back in darkness, poured into Troy and burned it to the ground.

THE LEGEND OF HEINRICH SCHLIEMANN

Heinrich Schliemann was born in Germany in 1822. As an eight-year-old, Heinrich loved the story of Troy and the wooden horse. He swore that when he grew up he would find and excavate the remains of this legendary city. Using descriptions in Homer's writing as a guide, Schliemann fulfilled his boyhood dream. He decided that the site of Troy wasn't at Bunarbashi where all the experts thought it was, but at Hisarlik, in what is now modern Turkey.

In the 1870s, he dug at Hisarlik, and found a city — rebuilt many times — with evidence that it had, indeed, been burnt to the ground on one occasion. He had found Troy, dumbfounded those who'd doubted him and also unearthed some fabulous treasures! These included a hoard of gold and silver, which Schliemann called Priam's Treasure, after the legendary King Priam of Troy.

THE TRUTH?

Throughout his life, Schliemann kept diaries and wrote thousands of letters. Despite this, there is no written record of him ever being interested in Troy until *after* he had visited Hisarlik. There he'd met a man called Frank Calvert, who actually owned some of the land the site was on. It was Calvert who was convinced that this was the site of Troy, and who probably aroused Schliemann's whole interest in the subject. Then there was the matter of Priam's Treasure. Schliemann claimed that he found it with his Greek wife Sophie. In fact, she wasn't even at Hisarlik on the day Schliemann claimed the gold and silver was unearthed!

Some of Schliemann's critics believe that he must have gathered together a number of unreported finds on the site to make up the hoard, because a report of one big find would cause much more excitement. Others claim that he actually brought the treasures from other archeological sites. Worst of all, some people believe that much of his so-called treasure was modern forgery.

Whatever the truth, Schliemann was widely respected by archeologists everywhere and became famous with the general public.

Sophie Schliemann modeling part of Priam's Treasure!

THE LEGEND OF LOST TREASURE

Schliemann died in 1890, leaving the collection of finds from Hisarlik — including Priam's Treasure — to a museum in Berlin. During the Second World War, the city was bombed many times, and rumors spread that the treasures had melted and poured down the museum steps in a river of gold. In fact, the Germans moved the treasure to the safety of a building at Berlin Zoo. After Berlin surrendered to the Russian forces, the Russians took the treasure to Moscow, where it is today. It is now on display in the Pushkin Museum, but both the Turkish and German governments claim that it is rightfully theirs.

IS IT REALLY TROY?

Did Schliemann really uncover Troy? The answer is, we just don't know. He did uncover a very important archeological site — an ancient city with at least eight different levels of occupation. This means that newer cities were built on top of earlier ones, layer after layer. The layer that Schliemann thought had been the Troy of Homer's epic poem was, it was later proved, to be of a different period. Whatever criticisms one has of Heinrich Schliemann, he certainly made the idea of archeology very exciting and his excavations captured the imagination of the world.

A fabulous golden vessel, also part of Priam's Treasure, c. 2300BC.

39

DISCOVERY

The supports on the south side of the Erechtheum at the Acropolis, shown above, are no ordinary columns. Shaped like women, they are called the "caryatids." But all is not what it seems. These are not the original carvings. They can be found in the Acropolis Museum and the British Museum.

This Roman statue is a copy of an Ancient Greek statue from the Hellenistic Age.

DISCOVERING THE PAST

Archeologists are people who study the past, by looking at things which have been left behind by earlier civilizations. Often they have to dig up these items first. Archeologists are the true History Detectives, piecing together clues left behind by ancient peoples. In this way, they build up a picture of how men, women and children might have lived before us. The influence of Ancient Greek life, art and technology is enormous and, having been taken up by the expanding Roman Empire, it has spread throughout the world.

ABSORBING TIMES

After the Romans conquered Ancient Greece, they copied everything from their statues to their temples, and developed many Greek ideas. In instances where few original Ancient Greek artifacts survive, studying the Roman copies often helps archeologists to build up a picture of Greek skills and techniques.

STORIES ON POTTERY

One of the most useful sources of information on Ancient Greece is pottery. Many fine examples of pots still survive, with decorative scenes that give a unique insight into what life was like in the Mediterranean thousands of years ago. There are two distinctive styles of Ancient Greek pot: black characters painted on red backgrounds called Black Attic, and red characters painted on black backgrounds, called Red Attic.

OUT OF THE PAGES OF LEGEND

One of the most famous of all Ancient Greek myths and legends is about the Minotaur, who was half bull, half man. He was said to have lived in a huge maze, called the Labyrinth, which was designed to trap the human sacrifices for him to catch and eat. The Labyrinth was supposed to be under the palace of his father, King Minos.

In 1900, on the island of Crete, the British archeologist Sir Arthur Evans discovered the remains of a palace at Knossos. The ruin was a maze of corridors and the symbol of the bull was found throughout the site. Whether the legend of the Minotaur grew from here, or the palace and bull-worship grew from the legend, no one knows. Although we have no idea what the people who lived there called themselves, Sir Arthur named the society "Minoan" after king Minos.

STOLEN OR SAVED?

In the past, some important ancient artifacts were taken from Greece, the most famous being the Elgin Marbles. Named after Lord Elgin, they are the beautifully carved stones that originally made up the frieze around the top of the Parthenon in Athens. Lord Elgin bought them from the Turks and took them to England at the beginning of the 19th century. He argued that they would be better preserved there, though this is still hotly disputed by some. The "marbles" are now housed in a special new exhibition space in the British Museum in London. The Greek government wants them back.

DISCOVERY

This bull's head *rhyton*, or ceremonial vase, was made by a Minoan craftsman in Crete. The Minoan palace of Knossos was topped with stylised bulls' horns, and a number of wallpaintings also contained images of bulls. This is why some people like to think that this could have been the actual palace of the legendary King Minos and his son, the Minotaur.

One of the Elgin Marbles, originally from the Parthenon. It is believed that they could have been carved to commemorate the battle of Marathon, when the Athenians beat a far bigger Persian army.

TIMELINE

The Greeks built many temples to their gods.

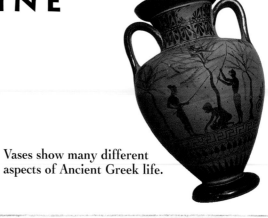

Vases show many different aspects of Ancient Greek life.

BC

c.2200BC–1450BC
MINOANS IN CRETE

c.1600BC–1100BC
MYCENAEANS ON MAINLAND GREECE

c.1250BC
A POSSIBLE DATE FOR THE TROJAN WAR
...IF IT REALLY HAPPENED!

c.1100BC–800BC
DARK AGES

c.800BC–500BC
ARCHAIC PERIOD
BIRTH OF THE CITY STATES

c.500BC
THE CLASSICAL PERIOD BEGINS
GOLDEN AGE OF ANCIENT GREECE

Prize athletes were honored and rewarded.

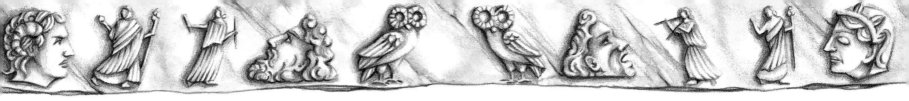

Greek foot soldiers were called *hoplites*.

431BC-404BC
PELOPONNESIAN WAR
BETWEEN SPARTA AND ATHENS

C.336BC
CLASSICAL PERIOD ENDS
HELLENISTIC AGE BEGINS
ALEXANDER THE GREAT
BECOMES KING OF MACEDONIA

323BC
ALEXANDER DIES IN BABYLON
HIS EMPIRE IS DIVIDED INTO
SEPARATE KINGDOMS

146BC
MACEDONIA AND GREECE FALL
UNDER ROMAN CONTROL

30BC
EGYPT, THE LAST HELLENISTIC
KINGDOM,
BECOMES PART OF THE
ROMAN EMPIRE
HELLENISTIC AGE ENDS

(C. = CIRCA, WHICH MEANS
APPROXIMATELY)

Aphrodite, Goddess of Love and Beauty.

The idea of theater came from Ancient Greece.

43

DEATH AT THE THEATER

A MYSTERY ADVENTURE STORY

YOUR MISSION

WELCOME TO THE CITY STATE OF ATHENS IN
ANCIENT GREECE. THINGS KEEP GOING WRONG
AT THE THEATER OF FOOLS, BUILT IN A SMALL TOWN
NOT FAR FROM ATHENS ITSELF. A NUMBER OF STRANGE
THINGS HAVE HAPPENED AND NOW THE ACTORS AND
CHORUS ARE BEGINNING TO WONDER IF THEY REALLY
ARE ACCIDENTS AFTER ALL. IS THE THEATER JINXED,
OR IS SOMEONE TRYING TO CAUSE SERIOUS TROUBLE?
IF SO, WHY?

IT'S UP TO YOU TO FIND OUT.

YOU'LL RECEIVE YOUR INSTRUCTIONS FROM THE
THEATER MANAGER, HAEMON.

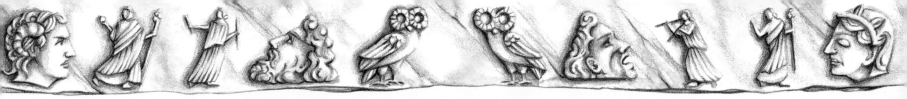

HOW TO BE A HISTORY DETECTIVE

To help you solve the mystery, you will need to answer questions along the way. These can be answered by using information from the first section of this book. Simply turn to the page number shown in the magnifying glass.

For example, would mean that an answer lay somewhere on page 12.

These answers also earn you points, so that you can keep score. You'll find how many points an answer scores when you check yours against the answers on pages 58 and 59.

But you must do more than simply answer the questions to find out who is causing trouble at the Theater of Fools. You must look out for clues in the words and pictures, too.

By the end of the story, you should be able to say who is up to no good and why. You can find out if you're right by checking page 60. The right solution will score you an extra 20 points.

Add up all your points and find out how good a history detective you are (also on page 60).

Good luck!

THE MAIN CHARACTERS

HAEMON
Manager of the Theater of Fools

SELENE
a theater musician

DOLIUS
Haemon's ancient assistant

MYRTILUS
an actor of many parts

GYAS
lead actor (with broken leg)

ALOPE
Gyas's daughter

PONTUS
actor and Gyas's understudy

THE SPARTAN
official investigator

YOUR MISSION BEGINS

Haemon, the theater manager, has arranged to meet you in the agora. "You start work tomorrow," he says, pausing by a stall to buy an apple. "Everyone at the theater will think you're the new stagehand," he tells you. "As far as they're concerned, your job is to help with the props and masks, and painting the scenery . . . What they won't know is that you're really on the lookout."

"On the lookout for what?" you ask eagerly.

"Anything and everything," he says.

"So far, we've had a mysterious fire backstage . . .

Gyas — my finest actor — has broken his leg . . .

and certain things have disappeared . . ."

"Why would anyone want to cause trouble at the Theater of Fools?" you ask.

Haemon shrugs. "Who knows? Our plays are meant to promote peace between different peoples, not trouble. You must find out."

"I'll do my best," you reassure him.

"I'll see you at the theater tomorrow. Remember, we must pretend to be meeting for the first time. You are to call yourself Belus." He says these last words as he hurries off through the crowds, leaving you by a fish stall.

"See that man?" you overhear a passer-by ask a fellow shopper. "That's Haemon. He used to be one of Athens's finest actors. He manages the Theater of Fools now."

"Where poor Gyas works? They could do with help from Asclepius!" replies the shopper.

What can she mean? 18

You arrive at the theater bright and early the next morning. There is a girl sweeping the circle of earth, called the orchestra, in front of the stage.

"Hello," she says. "You must be the new stagehand."

You nod. "My name's Belus," you say, using the false name Haemon gave you.

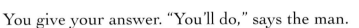

"I'm Alope," says the girl. "I don't really work here properly. I just like to help out. My dad's Gyas, the actor. Have you heard of him?"

You nod a second time. Suddenly Alope looks sad. "He's broken his leg . . . There's been a lot of bad luck around here lately."

"That's because the gods are angry," mutters an old man with a stern face. "Are you Belus?"

"Yes, sir," you reply, a little nervously.

"Ever worked in a theater before?" You shake your head. "Know what an *ekkyklema* is?" he asks.

You rack your brains for a reply. What is it? **27**

You give your answer. "You'll do," says the man. "Haemon is in charge here and I answer to him. The rest of you answer to me. Got that? My name is Dolius. Now follow me."

"Good luck on your first day," Alope smiles as you hurry off after Dolius.

Dolius keeps you busy for the next few hours, fetching and carrying and doing all the jobs no one else wants to do. You find something a bit like a coin dropped on the ground.

"You won't be able to buy much with that!" laughs Alope.

If it's not a coin, then what is it? **21**

It is late afternoon and a performance is about to start. Haemon sweeps past you, pretending not to know you.

"Listen everyone," he says. "I have bad news. Pontus, who was to play the lead role since Gyas broke his leg, hasn't shown up . . ."

There is a gasp among the performers. "So I will have to play the part myself, tonight."

"You can't!" protests Dolius. "You haven't acted for years!"

"But I must," says Haemon. "The show must go on!"

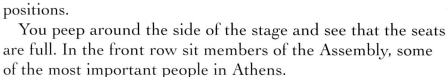

Despite mutterings of "more bad luck," "angry god" and "jinx" among the cast, the actors still take their positions.

You peep around the side of the stage and see that the seats are full. In the front row sit members of the Assembly, some of the most important people in Athens.

The chorus starts to chant from the orchestra below, Haemon pulls on his mask and marches on to the stage. The play is underway. You creep backstage to keep a lookout for anything unusual.

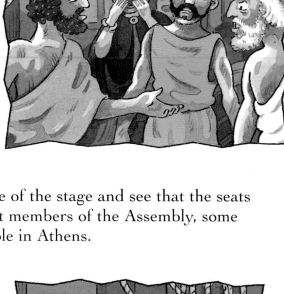

The musician Selene is standing by a strange-looking pulley system, rope in hand. You frown. What is it used for? 26

Selene moves away and you inspect the rope. It's been cut halfway through! This is obviously another carefully planned "accident," just waiting to happen.

Suddenly your thoughts are interrupted by a terrible cry of agony and a gasp from the audience. You swiftly run to the front of the stage and there Haemon lies bleeding on the ground, a knife thrust deep into his side.

"I am done for!" he groans as the mask is pulled from his face.

You can't believe it. Haemon is dead! The only one who knows that you aren't really a stagehand, but a detective, is *dead*.

"What a terrible thing," says Pontus, who has appeared at last. "If I hadn't been delayed by my son's *amphidromia*, that could have been me killed tonight."

What is an *amphidromia*? 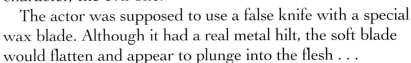 **36**

"It's Myrtilus I feel sorry for," says Selene. "He's the one who killed Haemon. What a dreadful, dreadful accident."

You piece together what is supposed to have happened in the play: Haemon's character, the peacemaker, is stabbed and wounded by Myrtilus's character, the evil one.

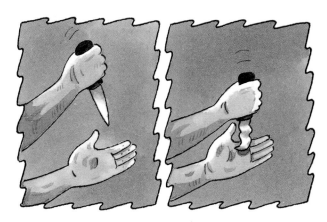

The actor was supposed to use a false knife with a special wax blade. Although it had a real metal hilt, the soft blade would flatten and appear to plunge into the flesh . . .

"And that was the knife I thought I was holding," wails Myrtilus, surrounded by his fellow performers. "It looked just like the one with the wax blade."

"This is the end of this play, I tell you. There shall be no more performances," cries Dolius. "I'm not staying a moment longer — the anger of the gods is upon us."

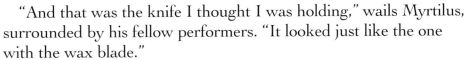

"No one is going anywhere unless I say so," booms a voice. You all turn around to see a large man standing on the edge of the stage.

"Who are you to give us orders?" demands Selene.

"They call me the Spartan," says the man. "I have been appointed by the Assembly members in the audience to act as official investigator."

"And how do you think you can help, Spartan?" asks Pontus, spitting out the last word like an insult. Why might the actor be hostile to the Spartan? **20**

WATCHING THE DETECTIVE

The shocked audience now gone, the Spartan orders you all up on to the stage. Alope, sobbing, clutches her father, Gyas's, hand.

"Who gave you the knife before you went on stage?" the Spartan asks Myrtilus.

"No one," replies the actor. "It was left on a table for me as usual to pick up and bring on."

"So any one of you could have swapped the knife with the wax blade for a real one," says

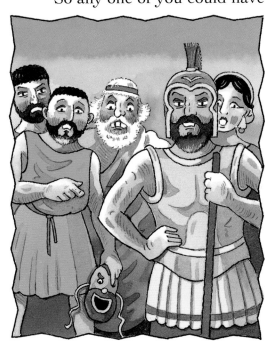

the Spartan, looking at us through narrowed eyes.

"Not me," protests Pontus. "I didn't arrive until Myrtilus was already on stage."

"Who would want to harm Haemon, anyway?" Selene interrupts. "If the Theater of Fools closes, we're out of a job. It must have been a terrible accident — some kind of mix up with the knives."

"Jobs or no jobs, I'm ending all performances!" announces Dolius. "Now that Haemon has . . . gone, I'm in charge and I say the gods have cursed this place!"

"You can't do that!" says Gyas, angrily. "You know Haemon always insisted that the show must go on —"

"QUIET!" orders the Spartan. "I will interview you each in turn." "Interrogate the new so-called stagehand," says Myrtilus, suddenly turning on you. "You're not what you seem, are you? I saw you by the *kyklos* talking in whispers to Haemon."

Suddenly, all eyes are turned in your direction. The *kyklos*? Where does Myrtilus mean? **32**

You insist that you'll only talk to the Spartan in private. He agrees and you explain who you really are and what you're really doing at the theater.

"All very interesting," says the investigator, "but the only person who can back up your story is now dead."

"I may not be able to prove I was hired by Haemon," you say, "but I can prove that I do a little detecting now and then." You give him the name of some satisfied clients.

"Very well," says the Spartan. "I'll check out your story but, until then, give you the benefit of the doubt. Keep up the pretence of being Belus, the stagehand, but you'll report back to me now, instead." You also tell him that you caught Selene by the rope that was cut halfway through.

Back among the performers, you sit with them around a long table, eating and drinking and watching them carefully.

"How long does he intend to keep us here?" fumes Selene. "I'm supposed to be helping to sew the dress of Athene in time for the Great Panathenaea." What's she talking about? 16

"Poor, poor Haemon," sighs Dolius. "Soon he'll be on his journey across the Styx." Where's that? 15

"All the more reason for keeping the Theater of Fools going, old man," protests Pontus. "In his memory."

"I'm not sure I'll ever act again," says Myrtilus, shakily, still eyeing you with suspicion.

Alope fills her father's cup with wine. He takes a sip then spits it out. "Poison!" he cries.

There is a gasp. Alope looks in the wine jar. It's not poison that's making the wine taste bad—there's something in the bottom of the jar! She puts in her hand and pulls out what's left of the knife with the wax blade.

The Spartan strides over. "So that's where the culprit hid the wax knife after the swap," he says.

"You think Haemon was murdered?" gasps Pontus.

"Yes," nods the Spartan. "But I think you were supposed to be the target, Pontus. The knives were switched but, because you were late, Haemon took your place and went on instead!"

"Otherwise it would have been me who ended up dead?" splutters Pontus in shock.

"Yes," nods the Spartan. "One of you here means this theater harm." He turns to the musician Selene. "Come with me. I have questions to ask you."

"I need protection!" Pontus cries, grabbing the Spartan. "I have a wife and three-week-old son. If anything should happen to me . . ."

"Pull yourself together," says Dolius. "You should go to the temple and thank the gods that your life was spared!"

"I will!" Pontus announces. "And no one can stop me!" He storms off. The Spartan looks at you and jerks his head in Pontus's direction. He wants you to follow him. You slip out after the actor. He's heading for the city, and you're hot on his heels.

Once in Athens, Pontus seems to be heading for a temple but, at the last moment, slips into a round building. What is it? 20

Moments later, the actor comes out with a man in armor. "Haemon dead?" says the soldier. "That changes everything. I can't talk now. Be at the Propylaea at sundown. And don't be late."

You decide to keep that appointment too.

Where is the Propylaea? 17

THE PLOT THICKENS

Hours later, as you make your way up to the Acropolis, you catch sight of some other familiar faces. They belong to Selene the musician and Myrtilus the actor.

"I'm sure that snooping stagehand Belus suspects me . . . I was standing by the rope cut halfway through," she says.

"It's the Spartan we've got to worry about," says Myrtilus. "If he thinks I deliberately switched knives and stabbed Haemon, I'm done for."

"Sssh!" says Selene. "That man in a himation is one of the *strategoi*!" Which man?

What's a himation? **34**   And who are the *strategoi*? **22**

You walk up to the Propylaea and, sure enough, there is Pontus lurking by a column. The man with the hat throws off his cape. It's the soldier who arranged to meet him.

"What now?" asks the actor.

"Who killed Haemon?" demands the soldier.

"Myrtilus stabbed him," says Pontus.

"Myrtilus is a murderer?" gasps the soldier.

"No one murdered Haemon," sighs Pontus.

"Not even you?" asks the soldier. "I know I told you to make sure the play was sto —"

"Sssh!" snaps Pontus. "There's someone eavesdropping!"

You think you've been found out, but it is Gyas's daughter Alope who is dragged out of the shadows.

"Little spies like you can get into big trouble," snarls the soldier.

Alope struggles to break free. "I heard every word!" she says, turning to Pontus. "You planned to stop the play going on, no matter what! It's your fault that my father broke his leg. You must have started the fire and murdered Haemon!"

"It's Gyas's daughter," says Pontus. "Everything's going wrong at once!"

The soldier grips Alope's arm. "If you believe anything you've just overheard, then believe this," he says urgently. "If Pontus says he didn't murder Haemon, then he didn't."

"Murderer!" shouts Alope, trying to break free.

"Hold on tight!" Pontus urges. "She's won at the Heraia before now." What can he mean by that? 🔍25

Somehow, Alope manages to break free and run off down the Acropolis. Pontus is about to chase after her.

"Let her go," says the soldier. "What harm can she do to us? The play has been abandoned, and your work is done. But, tell me, do you know who swapped the knife which killed Haemon?"

Pontus says nothing, but hands the soldier a paper scroll. "My report," he says. "Now, I must be gone."

The two men go their separate ways. You decide to follow the soldier and run slap bang into Gyas, sending his crutch flying.

"You fool," he says. "Watch where you're going . . ."

But you're not listening. You see that the scroll in the soldier's hand has brushed against a nail and torn . . . and a piece of the message is snagged on it. Apologizing to Gyas, you snatch the fragment of paper before it blows away, and read the words. What's a cithara? 🔍29

rope with that, then S came in looking for cithara and had to think fast and put the real knife down where the wax

"I've been busy too," says the Spartan, after you report to him everything you've seen and heard. "I've identified the knife that was swapped for the one with the wax blade. It didn't belong to the killer. It's one that's kept backstage for odd jobs . . . so a dead end there, I'm afraid."

Not necessarily . . . You wonder if one knife could be mistaken for another by someone other than Myrtilus on stage . . .

"I have, however, found out why certain people—such as the *strategos* you saw Pontus scheming with—might want to put a stop to the play," the Spartan continues. "Some Athenians think it tries too hard to promote friendship with us Spartans . . . but is this enough to murder a man for? It seems clear to me that Pontus has been behind the so-called accidents . . . but murder?"

You hand him your list of suspects. "I think I know who killed Haemon," you say. "At the Theater of Fools, things are not always what they seem."

You can check your answer with the SOLUTION on page 60

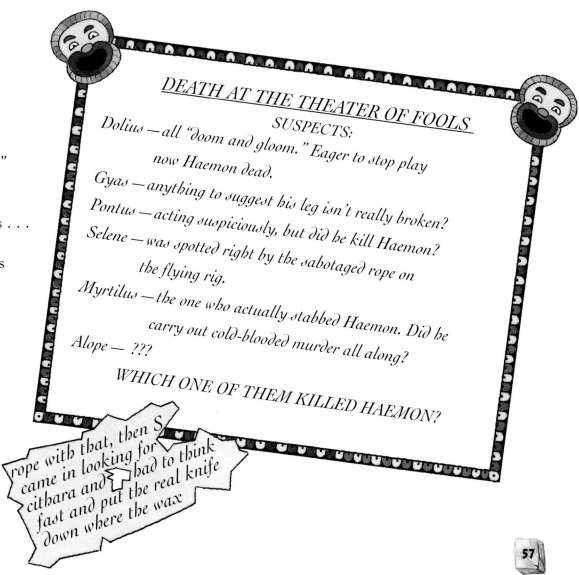

DEATH AT THE THEATER OF FOOLS
SUSPECTS:

Dolius — all "doom and gloom." Eager to stop play now Haemon dead.

Gyas — anything to suggest his leg isn't really broken?

Pontus — acting suspiciously, but did he kill Haemon?

Selene — was spotted right by the sabotaged rope on the flying rig.

Myrtilus — the one who actually stabbed Haemon. Did he carry out cold-blooded murder all along?

Alope — ???

WHICH ONE OF THEM KILLED HAEMON?

rope with that, then S came in looking for cithara and had to think fast and put the real knife down where the wax

ANSWERS AND SCORES

Next to each answer is a number. This is the number of points you should award yourself if you got the answer right without looking it up here in the back first. And there are extra points if you worked out who is behind the death of Haemon, Manager of the Theater of Fools.

PAGES 48 & 49

- The shoppers have obviously heard about Gyas's broken leg. Asclepius is the god of healing!   5 points

- An *ekkyklema* is a kind of "bed" which characters killed off-stage could be wheeled in on, in Ancient Greek theater.   5 points

- It's a ballot disc, of the type used by jurors when they think a person is innocent.   5 points

PAGES 50 & 51

- It is part of the pulley system for the "flying rig," a wooden framed crane used to make actors' characters appear to fly.   5 points

- The *amphidromia* is a baby's naming ceremony, ten days after its birth.   6 points

- Spartans are the people of Sparta, a city state often at war with Athens. We know that the Theater of Fools is just outside the city of Athens, so some of the performers might see Spartans as natural enemies.   6 points

PAGES 52 & 53

- The *kyklos* is the slave market platform in the agora. Myrtilus must have witnessed your meeting with Haemon the day before.   6 points

- The dress of Athene is a giant dress hung like a sail on a ceremonial ship, carried at the Athens festival of Great Panathenaea.   5 points

- According to Ancient Greek beliefs, the soul's journey to the underworld — to begin the afterlife — took it across a river called the Styx.   5 points

PAGES 54 & 55

- The building is a Tholos — meeting place of the Council.   5 points
- The Propylaea is the gateway to the sacred enclosure on the
  Acropolis in Athens.   6 points
- When worn by a man, a himation is a garment wrapped around the
  body with the end thrown over a shoulder — rather like a Roman toga.
  The only man wearing one here is the person with the hat.   5 points
- The *strategoi* are the commanders of the Athenian army.
  (A single commander is called a *strategos*.)   6 points

PAGES 56 & 57

- The Heraia was a sports event for women and girls, made up of three
  types of races. If Alope has won one, she must be a fast runner.   5 points
- A cithara is a musical instrument, rather like a harp or lyre.   5 points

A MESSAGE TO ALL WOULD-BE HISTORY DETECTIVES

Add up your score so far, before you turn the page
to find out who is behind the death of Haemon. . .

When you've checked the solution, score an extra
10 points if you guessed the right person.

Score **20 points** if you worked out who the spy
was by spotting all the clues.

SOLUTION

A number of performers at the Theater of Fools have been acting suspiciously. You spotted Selene by the cut rope (page 50), and her conversation with Myrtilus on the way to the Acropolis (page 55) is interesting — but there's nothing to say it was she who actually cut the rope, and the conversation could have been an innocent discussion about the fear of being wrongly accused.

Gyas's understudy, Pontus, is the performer who has been behaving the most strangely. From a conversation you overheard him having with the soldier (page 56), it's obvious that he's been trying to stop the play, for reasons outlined by the Spartan (page 57). But is that enough for him to kill Haemon?

Pontus said that he'd been delayed because he was at his son's *amphidromia* — a baby-naming ceremony which is ten days after a child's birth (page 51). But he later told the Spartan that his son was three weeks old (page 54) — which means the *amphidromia* would have been about eleven days ago.

He also told the Spartan that he arrived after Myrtilus had gone on stage with the knife, so he couldn't have been the person who swapped it for a real one — but Pontus is the masked man standing behind Myrtilus before the play has even started (page 50).

Although his face is hidden by the mask, his bracelet is a giveaway. It matches the bracelet he can clearly be seen wearing throughout the rest of the adventure. He is wearing the same cloak in the background (on page 50) as the one at the Propylaea (pages 55 and 56).

There is also a clue to suggest it was Pontus who dropped the knife with the wax blade in the jar of wine. The first time we see the jar, it has a stopper in it to keep the wine fresh (page 51). The next time we see the same jar, the stopper is missing (page 51). The object Pontus is holding on stage (page 52) is, in fact, the jar stopper!

The conversation you and Alope heard between the soldier and Pontus at the Propylaea (pages 55 and 56). It not only strongly suggested that Pontus was, indeed, behind the "accidents" at the theater, but also that he did not murder Haemon. In fact, he went so far as to say "no one murdered Haemon."

But how does he know that?

Because it was an accident. The part of Pontus's report, torn off by a nail (page 56), helps explain the final piece of the puzzle. In it, Pontus says that someone "came in looking for" their "cithara and . . . [hole in paper] . . . without thinking put the real knife down where the wax . . ." A cithara is the kind of musical instrument Selene had under her arm when you saw her by the cut rope backstage.

So here's what happened: Pontus, in disguise, sneaked backstage to cut the rope to the flying crane. He picked up a knife to cut it, only to break the wax blade and realize that it was a prop! He found another knife and was cutting the rope when he heard Selene coming. Not wanting to be caught with the knife in his hand, he quickly put it down on the table where the wax-blade prop knife had been. Myrtilus then picked the real knife up and, thinking it had a harmless wax blade, stabbed Haemon on stage, killing him. Pontus had indeed caused the theater manager's death, but he hadn't planned it. In fact, it wasn't murder. It was the only true accident at the Theater of Fools.

HOW DID YOU DO?

BETWEEN 90 AND 100 POINTS Wow! When it comes to being a History Detective, you're the very best. You're not only good at following the clues, but you worked them all out brilliantly. Well done. **BETWEEN 75 AND 89 POINTS** Excellent! You're true detective material. You worked well with the facts to solve the clues. **BETWEEN 60 AND 74 POINTS** Not bad. Not bad at all. You've got some way to go before you're a truly great detective, but you certainly know how to handle an investigation. **BETWEEN 50 AND 59 POINTS** OK, so you're not going to win any big-shot detective awards, but you're on your way to becoming a pretty good detective. Keep practicing! **LESS THAN 50 POINTS** Oh dear. A short spell at detective school wouldn't do any harm. Better luck next time!

GLOSSARY

Agora — market place and meeting place in the middle of a Greek city, usually surrounded by public buildings and shops.

Aristocrat — a person from a rich family of landowners (from the Greek *aristoi* meaning "best people").

Assembly — a regular meeting of citizens in Athens, debating proposals from the Council and voting on them.

Caryatid — a column carved to look like a woman or goddess.

Chiton — a woman's one-piece dress, fastened at the shoulder.

Chorus — performers who sang, danced and commented on action in a play.

Citizens — free men with the right to play a part in governing a city state.

City State — or *polis* (plural, *poleis*), an independent Greek state, made up of a city and its surrounding countryside.

Council — a group of 500 councillors in Athens, who processed and worded policies and laws, suggested by citizens, to put before the Assembly.

Democracy — from the Greek *demos* meaning "people" and *kratos* meaning "rule."

Hoplite — a heavily armed foot soldier fighting for any one of the city states' armies.

Mystery Cult — a religion with secret rituals, only attended by worshippers specially initiated into the cult.

Paidagogos — a slave whose job it was to go to school with a boy and make sure he did his lessons properly.

Phalanx — a battle formation of *hoplites*, eight ranks deep.

Relief — a carving that stands out against a flat background on a slab of stone.

Rhapsode — a professional reciter of poetry at parties and festivals.

Slaves — an unpaid servant, with no rights and "owned" by someone else.

Strategos — one of ten army commanders in the Athenian city state, elected each year. *Strategoi* carried out policies agreed by the Council and Assembly.

Tyrant — an unelected ruler who exercised absolute power, like a dictator. (The word is now used to describe cruel, powerful leaders anywhere.)

INDEX